THE

with FREDDIE FACEOFF and FANNY FACE

ICE MONSTER

Text by Alias Smith
Sport Mites characters created and illustrated by Bob Pelkowski

BARRON'S
New York ● London ● Toronto ● Sydney
Text and illustrations ©1989 by MITEY CLUBHOUSE ADCO LTD. All rights reserved.
No part of this book may be reproduced or copied in any
form without written permission from the copyright owner.
ISBN 0-8120-4243-3
PRINTED IN HONG KONG

"Come on, Redbert. Can we see if the ice on the pond is safe?" Sport Mites Fanny Falls and Freddie Faceoff urged the bright red bird perched on top of the Mitey Clubhouse. "We're ready to have some fun!"

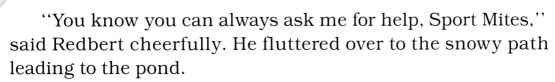

"You know you can always ask me for help, Sport Mites," said Redbert cheerfully. He fluttered over to the snowy path leading to the pond.

Fanny straightened her hockey helmet as Freddie gathered their equipment.

"Here's your stick," Freddie said. "I'll carry the puck."

"Let's go!" Fanny and Freddie shouted enthusiastically. They wobbled along the path on their skates, eagerly following Redbert.

"We're almost there," Redbert said. "I'll fly ahead and make sure you can skate on the pond."

"How's the ice?" Freddie hollered.

He and Fanny went up to Redbert, who was busily brushing snow off a big sign near the pond.

"You were right to check before playing here," Redbert said. "See—the Park Safety Patrol put this sign up saying the ice is safe."

"I knew it!" Freddie grinned.

"Thanks, Redbert," Fanny said.

"I have a few things to do at the Mitey Clubhouse," said Redbert as he flew up and circled the pond. "Then I'll come back and watch you play. See you soon."

As they waved good-bye to their friend, Freddie's and Fanny's faces gleamed with excitement like the dancing sunbeams on the glistening ice.

"We have the *whole* pond to ourselves," Freddie said, tossing the hockey puck on the ice.

The two friends carefully stepped on the ice.

"Fanny, you have to keep your stick close to the ice and hold it with two hands. Watch me." Freddie showed Fanny how far along the stick to put each of her hands.

"That makes me bend over," Fanny said.

"It helps you balance while you're skating," Freddie said. "But you should also bend your knees. Now, spread your skates apart and point them straight ahead."

"Like this?" asked Fanny.

"Perfect," said Freddie. "Now you look like a real hockey player."

"You can skate over to one of the nets," Freddie instructed Fanny. "I'll skate with the puck first and try to get it into the net for a goal."

"You'd better try hard!" Fanny challenged. "I'm not letting you get a point!"

Moving the puck back and forth with his stick as he skated, Freddie brought the puck close to the net.

With his head up and his eyes on the puck, Freddie snapped his wrists.

The puck flew toward the net.

Fanny tried to stop it from going into the net. CLUNK!

The puck missed the net, hit the post, and went sailing through the air.

"Can we play?" asked a voice.

"Who said that?" Freddie asked suspiciously as he and Fanny looked all around the pond.

"I did," said the voice. "I'm Scooter."

"And I'm Jacques."

Scooter and Jacques climbed over the snowbank where they had been watching Fanny and Freddie.

"I'm Freddie Faceoff and this is Fanny Falls."

"But she's a girl!" groaned Jacques.

"Girls can play hockey, too," Fanny said with a toss of her head.

"Well, then may we play with you?" asked Jacques, more politely this time.

"Maybe," answered Freddie. "But first we have to find our hockey puck!"

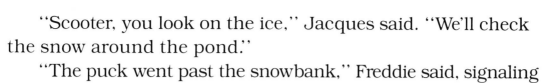

"Scooter, you look on the ice," Jacques said. "We'll check the snow around the pond."

"The puck went past the snowbank," Freddie said, signaling the others to follow him. "I think it landed over on this side. See—there it is! But what—"

Freddie froze.

"Scooter! Come quick!" Jacques shouted, crouching beside Freddie, who was staring at some strange marks in the snow.

"What's the matter?" gasped Scooter.

"Look! What are they?" asked Jacques.

"Monster tracks for sure," Freddie whispered, swiftly grabbing the hockey puck.

"How can you tell?" asked Fanny.

"I just know," said Freddie. "It's not a dog or a cat. The prints are too big."

"What should we do?" asked Jacques.

"Hello, Sport Mites," Redbert said, startling everyone as he landed on the snowbank.

"Redbert! Look at these marks!" Freddie and Fanny cried
out.

"Hmmmmm," said Redbert. "Looks like a strange
creature, all right. And it's heading towards the Clubhouse. I'll
just get my snowshoes and see if I can track it down. Leave it
to me, Sport Mites. Go and have fun now. I'll be right back."

"Who's the bird?" asked Jacques as the little group returned to the pond.

"Redbert is our friend. He looks after all the Sport Mites at the Mitey Clubhouse," Fanny said.

"Can Jacques and I be Sport Mites?" asked Scooter.

"Sure," answered Freddie. "Just meet us one day at the Mitey Clubhouse over there and I'll tell you all about that."

"What about the monster?" Scooter asked nervously.

"Redbert knows what to do," Fanny said confidently.

"Anyhow," said Freddie, "now that we've found our puck, let's play!"

Freddie dropped the puck on the ice beside Jacques.

"You know, in real games each team has five players, plus a goalie who tries to keep the puck out of the net," said Jacques.

"We know," said Freddie. "But this is pond hockey. We can play just for fun."

"How about Fanny and you against Scooter and me?"
Jacques asked.

"Good!" agreed Freddie.

Fanny and Scooter skated toward their nets.

"Don't let Jacques get a goal," Freddie called out to Fanny.
"I can tell he wants to score a point."

Jacques and Freddie put the puck on the ice between them and each tried to hit it. Freddie won the face-off! He skated left and then right, pushing the puck with his stick. Jacques chased after Freddie, trying to get the puck away as Freddie weaved his way toward Scooter.

"Over here, Freddie," Fanny shouted.

Freddie watched Fanny come out of the net and glide by to help him. Jacques and Scooter watched her, too.

Scooter skated over to Jacques.

Freddie stopped. He passed the puck to Fanny.

"Get into the net," Jacques shouted to Scooter.

Scooter scrambled frantically to the net as Jacques raced across the ice toward the puck. Meanwhile, Fanny slapped the puck with her stick.

"Oh no!" Scooter wailed as he slid and slipped on the ice.

"Goal!" cheered Freddie, as Fanny's shot zipped into the net.

"That's all right, Scooter," Jacques said as he helped his friend up. "We'll have plenty of chances to score ourselves!"

CRUNCH! CRUNCH!

"Do you hear what I hear?" asked Freddie.

CRUNCH! CRUNCH! CRUNCH! CRUNCH!

"It's the monster!" Scooter gasped. "I'm scared!"

CRUNCH! CRUNCH! CRUNCH! CRUNCH!

"We'll have to be quiet. Monsters can be dangerous," whispered Freddie.

"Where's your friend Redbert?" whispered Jacques.

"Maybe he's fighting the monster," whispered Fanny.

Mustering all their courage, the four friends crept over to the snowbank.

"Let's take a peek," whispered Fanny.

CRUNCH!   CRUNCH!

"The only way to chase the monster with these snowshoes, is to stay on the ground," Redbert thought, landing once again.
CRUNCH! CRUNCH!
HEE! HEE!
"What's that noise?" said Redbert suspiciously. "It must be the monster . . . but monsters don't giggle and laugh!"

The four friends tumbled merrily over the snowbank in front of Redbert.

"Oh, Redbert! See the marks your snowshoes made!" chuckled Freddie. "*You're* the ice monster!"

Redbert laughed, too. "So I am!" he said, his eyes twinkling. "I must have made those tracks when I checked the ice earlier this morning, before you came by. I bet I'm the only ice monster trying to protect his best friends from himself!"

HOCKEY RI■

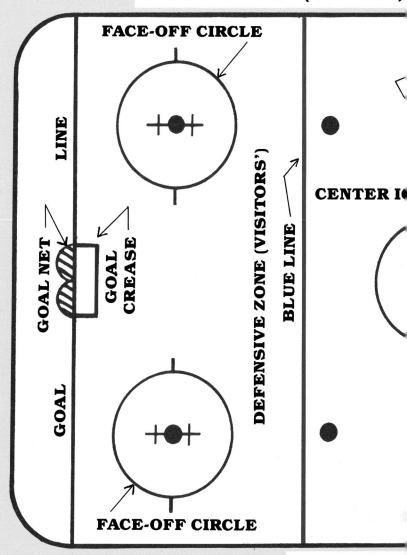

PLAYERS' BENCH (VISITORS)

FACE-OFF CIRCLE

LINE

GOAL NET

GOAL CREASE

GOAL

DEFENSIVE ZONE (VISITORS')

BLUE LINE

CENTER I■

FACE-OFF CIRCLE

PENALTY BO

DIAGRAM

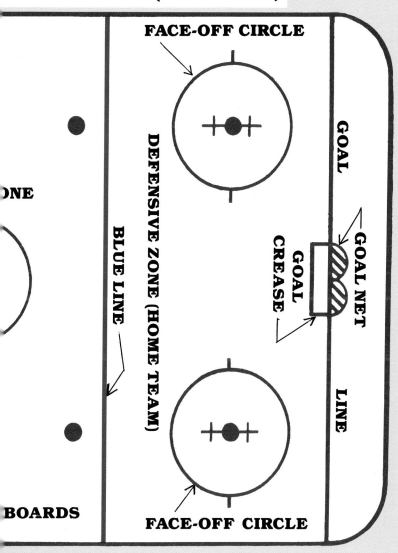

FACE-OFF CIRCLE

DEFENSIVE ZONE (HOME TEAM)

BLUE LINE

ZONE

BOARDS

FACE-OFF CIRCLE

GOAL

GOAL NET

GOAL CREASE

LINE

Hockey Terms

ice hockey   A game played between two six-player teams skating on ice. Each player has a hockey stick and uses it to move the hockey puck around the hockey rink.

helmet   A hard plastic head covering, usually with a face mask, to protect the player's head from injury.

hockey puck   A hard rubber disk that slides across the ice as it is hit with a hockey stick.

net   A woven cord or plastic mesh attached to a frame and positioned at the end of the hockey rink.

goal   The action of hitting the hockey puck into the net for one point.

hockey team   A team of six skating players. The team positions are: one goalie, who protects the net area; two wingers who play offense; two defensive players and one center.

face-off   The action of dropping the puck between two opposing players, usually by the referee, to start the game or to continue the game action after it has been stopped.

pass   The action of moving the hockey puck from one player to a teammate by slapping, pushing, or tapping the puck with the hockey stick.

shot   The action of trying to score a goal.

hockey stick   A wooden or plastic flat stick with a long shaft. The stick has a corner bend at the bottom called a blade, which is used to hit the hockey puck on the ice.